Becoming Shooters

A Guide for New Gun Owners

Dustin P. Salomon

and

Innovative Services and Solutions LLC

Silver Point, Tennessee

Thank you for purchasing this book.

If you care about gun safety as much as we do, please visit the website below to access our free video series on safety and fundamental gun handling.

https://www.buildingshooters.com/free

This program contains some of the most important skills anyone who uses firearms will ever learn.

Yet these same skills are still frequently ignored in formal programs of instruction, leading to many avoidable accidents.

Join us in working to make the firearms industry, and society in general, a safer place. Secure your access now.

CONTENTS

SECTION I:

ALL ABOUT GUN SAFETY

Even if you *loathe* guns, please take the time to learn this life saving information.

Understanding it <u>will</u> make you, and everyone around you, safer.

CHAPTER ONE:

SAFETY — THE ONLY THING YOU NEED TO LEARN

B efore we discuss anything else, I want to talk about gun safety. This is, by far, the most important topic in this book. Guns, when combined with ammunition, are inherently dangerous tools. Even ignoring intentional acts of violence, too many accidents happen every year — over 16,000 in the United States. *All* of these can be prevented with the application of some very basic principles.

Different people take different approaches to safety. For reasons that I will explain later in this book, I am going to introduce you to what I believe is the simplest, most effective approach. It is based upon just two fundamental rules. If you remember nothing else from this book — even if you do not read one more page of it—please take the time both to finish this Chapter and to understand fully the information that is on it. Even if you despise the subject matter, your knowledge of this information has the potential to save a life someday. It is that important!

The first rule is to **know where the muzzle** (the part that the bullets come out of) **is pointed**, and to **point it in the safest direction** intentionally. This generally means that if the gun were to fire a bullet at any given moment in time, the direction that the muzzle is pointed in would provide the *least* chance of killing or injuring someone among the directions available.

The second rule is to **know where the trigger of the gun is**. This is usually a slightly curved lever that makes the gun fire when it is pressed. **Never <u>touch</u> the trigger** unless you intend, or are willing, to fire a real bullet in the direction that the muzzle is pointed.

If you fully understand, and can apply, what was written in this Chapter and choose not to read further, I still consider this book a success. If not, please at least read Chapter Three. In it these two rules are explained in detail. Even if you *loathe* guns, please do take the time to learn this life saving information. Understanding it <u>**will**</u> make you, and everyone around you, safer.

Chapter Two:

Introduction

This book is intended for new gun owners, new shooters, and persons who are interested in, or curious about, purchasing or owning a firearm. I am therefore assuming that you fall into one of these categories and are not readily familiar with the subject matter. It may interest you to know that twenty-five years ago, there was very little information readily available about the subject of firearms training. The internet, as we know it today, did not exist and most highly skilled and experienced shooters and trainers preferred to keep most of their in-depth knowledge about shooting out of the mainstream.

For better or for worse, today the opposite is true. There is an overwhelming volume of content available on firearms and tactical training that includes books, blogs, videos, and websites. There is also an ever-increasing number of tactical training facilities and instructors who are ready and willing to provide training.

Many of these instructors and providers of content are very good, as are many of the sources of information about equipment, skill performance and tactics. It is not my intent to parse through them here, nor do I want to add yet one more book covering the same subject matter to the mix.

It is instead my intent to add something unique to the voluminous body of information that is now available to new shooters, specifically, *how to learn*. There is much out there that is of value but, as you will see, much of it is presented to you in ways that make learning it much more difficult than it needs to be.

As with any subject, and especially any subject related to firearms, one of the first questions that you should always ask is why you should listen to the person who is speaking. Therefore, an entirely reasonable question that you should be asking yourself is why you should care about, or listen to, anything I have to say.

I am not a high-level competitive shooter. I am not a former police officer, nor a special forces operator. Therefore, before we get into the "meat and potatoes," allow me to share some of my background and a few of the experiences that led to me writing this book.

I am a former naval officer, graduate of the U.S. Naval Academy, and formerly worked as a full-time security professional in war-time Iraq and other high-threat overseas locations. When I was growing up, guns were always present in the house. My father was a career FBI Agent who spent most of his years in The Bureau working on various SWAT teams. Starting from an early age, he taught me basic firearms safety, as well as how to shoot.

While at the Naval Academy, I went through the standard firearms training and qualification during Plebe Summer (the Naval Academy's "boot camp" equivalent). Later during my first year, I had the opportunity to try out for, and became a member of, the Navy Combat Pistol Team. This provided me with the opportunity to learn shooting from some incredible mentors from the U.S. Marine Corps and Naval Special Warfare (Navy SEAL) communities.

This experience also gave me my first view into how much I probably should have learned (but never did). This is from both when I was growing up and during Plebe Summer, during training that was very similar to what is still considered a standard approach to military, security, and law enforcement firearms training and qualification.

I entered the Naval Fleet just a few months prior to the terrorist attack on the *USS Cole* in Yemen, and a few years prior to the September 11, 2001 terrorist attacks on the World Trade Center and Pentagon. These two events caused seismic shifts in the military's mission and overall state of readiness. In the Navy specifically, they caused very significant changes to how security operations and firearms training were implemented.

Because of my personal interests, experiences with firearms, and prior firearms training, I was assigned to positions where I had the opportunity to lead the development of two navy security forces, as well as the firearms and tactical training to support them. After leaving the Navy in 2004, I continued working as an armed professional for nearly a decade, supporting the global war on terror.

Because of my background and personal experiences, my interests and passion lean towards improving methods of armed workforce development and management. As a junior officer, I was tasked with preparing roughly 80 sailors to go to war. I was then repeatedly told, "No," when I tried to get them what I thought was the training and equipment necessary to accomplish that task at a reasonable level.

This was incredibly frustrating. It also left me with a burning desire to find better ways to do things. I do not believe that any person should be sent to do an incredibly dangerous job, risking his or her life, while being prepared with training that is both demonstrably ineffective and obviously irrelevant to the job requirements of the real world. Nevertheless, this is the situation in which many, possibly even most, armed professionals find themselves.

These experiences led me down the winding road of discovery. I spent the better part of two decades researching ways to improve training. What I eventually learned is that the problems I was trying to solve are rooted in something far more fundamental than shooting techniques or tactics. These subjects are important; however, they are not where we have a systemic issue in the industry. The real problems are instead based in how the human brain works — and in how we fail to consider this when we design and deliver training.

While clearly my personal focus (and that of my company, Building Shooters) is on the needs of armed professionals, it is an indisputable fact that these same issues impact every segment of the industry, and every person who owns and uses firearms. It does not matter whether that person is a combat-seasoned Delta Force commando, a police officer, a security guard, a yuppie in an office building, a housewife in the suburbs, or a millennial doing social media marketing from a coffee shop. We all have the same basic brain structure and the same basic brain functions. Anything fundamental enough to be rooted in how the brain works impacts all of us.

The training problems that I have been working on solving for now over twenty years are highly relevant for civilians and nowhere is this truer than for entry-level gun owners and shooters who are trying to "learn the ropes". Unfortunately, the way in which entry-level training within the industry is usually delivered does not do the average person many favors.

As I will explain in the second section of this book, the industry-standard approach is to deliver training in ways that can actively *impede* a student's future ability to develop as a shooter. In some cases, these training methods can even hinder a person's ability to develop what I consider to be minimally adequate gun-handling and self-defense skills. It is for this reason that I have written this book.

This state-of-affairs is tragic, and not just because of the impact it has on the shooting community, and society at large. (Face it, more than 16,000 avoidable gun accidents per year is simply not an acceptable statistic. We can do better.) The tragedy is compounded because some of the "harm" being inflicted on students is done by instructors who genuinely and passionately care about providing the best training possible — and because it is entirely avoidable.

This book is part of a much broader effort by Building Shooters to influence an industry-wide reversal of this unfortunate state-of-affairs. The book's contents will be largely repetitive for anyone who has read, especially, my 2017 book *Mentoring Shooters*. Unlike my other writing, however, this book is not written for experienced shooters or instructors. Its intended audience is at the entry level of the industry.

To my intended reader: the information contained in these pages will help you safely and successfully navigate your way into this increasingly complex industry. It will also help you safely and effectively integrate the capability of a firearm into your life. The objective of this book is to help you efficiently and effectively achieve the knowledge and skill necessary to handle a gun safely, defend yourself and your family if necessary and, if you so desire, advance rapidly in your skills for sport, recreation, competitive, defensive, or professional reasons.

CHAPTER THREE:

THE GUN SAFETY RULES

It is impossible to overemphasize gun safety. However, that never stops me from trying and I hope that you will inherit this trait. Firearms add to, and equalize, individual physical capability in ways that no other tool can. They are also inherently dangerous and unforgiving.

I am a strong believer in the importance of an individual right to bear arms. It is, fundamentally, the only true personal equalizer in a free society. When afforded personal arms, we are all equally physically capable at applying force. It is an undeniable fact that application of force is an omnipresent feature of human society. Some people are naturally gifted at it, through factors such as size and strength. Others are denied much capability at all. However, with the right to bear arms, we are all afforded the opportunity to truly achieve physical equality where it really matters.

It is also important to acknowledge that this capability is derived from the fact that firearms are inherently dangerous tools that have the potential to be terribly unforgiving. You cannot call back a bullet once it has been fired — no matter how much you might wish you could. There are no do-overs.

While it is important to respect firearms, and the capabilities they bring, it is also important not to *fear* them. Guns and ammunition are simply inanimate objects. They are neither good nor bad. They are simply tools that have both capabilities and limitations — like any other tools ranging from hammers, to bleach, to motor vehicles.

The keys are knowledge, skill, and intent. You must know both how the tool works and how to use it. Then, and only then, will a gun be useful to help you improve your own safety. It is not the gun that makes you safer. It is you — using the capability of the gun correctly — that does so.

I am not going to write a detailed guide to administrative gun handling in this book. If you are looking for this level of detail, my book *Mentoring Shooters* has a written step-by-step guide, with detailed pictures, for administrative gun handling and safety (with semiautomatic pistols). A video series that is available for free at https://www.buildingshooters. com/free also contains very detailed instructions and examples, with real students, of how to learn the basics of safe gun handling. I highly encourage you to access and take advantage of these resources.

What I *am* going to do in this book is discuss the concepts of gun safety at a very general level. My objective is to drill down and distill gun safety to the few concepts that truly are critical, regardless of whether you are a gun owner or not.

The gun safety model I am introducing in this book is a little bit different than what you may see in other places, such as your local range, gun store, or firearms training facility (more on this in the next Chapter). This is not because anybody else is doing anything wrong, or because those other methods cannot be used effectively. Instead, this is because, as a trainer, I try to base everything around the twin factors of how the brain works and what the end goal of the training is — usually defined by real-world needs.

The human brain is an incredibly advanced information processing system (more on this in Section 2). It also has some limitations that can bite us if we do not consider them when we train. For example, the average person's brain is only capable of handling about seven pieces of information at any given time. We are incredibly poor at effective multi-tasking and are generally only able to accomplish one complex task at a time with any degree of success.

Our brains are also limited in how much conscious information they can process during any specific timeframe. This is very important to consider when it comes to using guns, not just under potentially stressful or life-threatening conditions, but also in situations where distractions that compromise our ability to concentrate on one specific thing may exist.

For most people in the modern world, this state of distraction exists *all of the time* — in every setting. Therefore, everything we do with guns, and gun safety, has a greater chance of succeeding if it *does not* require significant conscious thought in the moment. The simpler things are, the better.

For this reason (and others that are outside the scope of this book) I recommend a gun safety model that is built on only two very simple rules. These rules always apply, in every setting or environment. It does not matter whether you are handling a gun for the first time, supervised, in a gun store or if you are a seasoned SWAT Team member making entry for the one-thousandth time on a high-risk warrant. These rules *always* apply.

Fundamental knowledge: Basic Gun Anatomy

Before you can hope to understand and apply the rules of gun safety, you first must understand just a little bit about how guns work and a few of their basic parts. It is likely that you already know what I am going to describe here, even if just from watching television or movies. However, because these things are so elemental to understanding gun safety, I am going to take the time to describe them here. Please bear with me if this information is already familiar to you.

In its simplest form, a gun is nothing more than a tool to launch projectiles. The vast majority of guns (including air guns and airsoft guns) work by using compressed gas to push a projectile through a tube at high velocity. When the projectile reaches the end of the tube, it launches and becomes airborne. *Firearms* work as a direct result of gunpowder, an accelerant, or fast-burning substance, (often incorrectly mistaken for an explosive) that rapidly turns from solid to gas after it has been ignited. In modern firearms this usually occurs via mechanical means such as being impacted by a spring activated pin inside the gun.

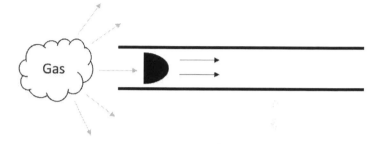

Figure 1 – Rapidly expanding gas pushes the projectile forward

There is of course more involved than this in making firearms work effectively. However, if you understand that expanding gas pushes a projectile, also called a *bullet*, forward down a tube then you understand the essence of it.

From a safety standpoint, (always the most important thing when dealing with firearms and other types of guns) this should leave two questions very clear:

1) What direction is the tube, also called the *barrel*, pointed in? This is important because, wherever the barrel is pointed, the bullet will go.

2) What makes the gas expand and how can this

process be controlled? In virtually all firearms this process is controlled mechanically via a lever that is commonly called a *trigger*. Pushing on this lever releases the gas. The expanding gas, in turn, pushes the projectile down the tube and launches it into the air.

If you want to control what happens with a gun (of any type), there are two things that you must be able to both identify and control. The first is the barrel (tube). The second is the trigger (lever). *If you can identify and control both the barrel and the trigger, then you can assure the safety of a gun at any given moment in time.*

While this may seem absurdly rudimentary, the ability to identify both the *muzzle* (the end of the barrel where the bullet will exit) and the *trigger* of a gun is the first part of gun safety. You *must* know what these are, and *where* they are, or you cannot hope to ensure that they are controlled appropriately and effectively.

Let us examine these in order or priority. First, the muzzle. There is no magic here. The muzzle is the end of the tube. It is the end the bullets will come out of when the gun is fired. You can be certain that the direction the muzzle is pointed in is the direction that the bullet will travel.

Figure 2 – The arrow points to the muzzle of a shotgun

Identifying the muzzle is a simple task; however, somewhat less simple is sometimes navigating and controlling the muzzle. The reason that the muzzle is important is because the direction it is pointed in indicates the exact area that is in potential danger, should the gun be fired. While identifying, moving, moving around, or otherwise interacting with a gun in any setting it is generally a best practice to ensure that neither people, nor property of consequence, are ever in the area that the muzzle is pointed towards.

Please do note, however, that on many public shooting ranges, shooters will move forward of the firing line and, therefore, in front of the muzzles of weapons in order to place, check, and repair targets. In these instances, there is generally a formal process of individually inspecting each gun to ensure that it is unloaded. There is also a prohibition on any person approaching or touching a gun while people are "down range."

These are standard practices and I consider them to be a perfectly safe and acceptable method of range management. The risks are both acknowledged by all parties and mitigated through the application of formal processes and procedures.

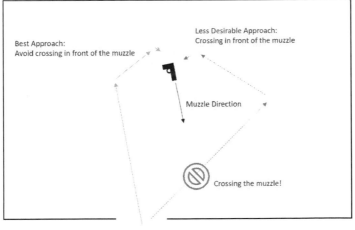

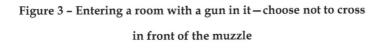

Figure 3 – Entering a room with a gun in it — choose not to cross in front of the muzzle

The second item of consideration is the trigger. This lever is typically located between the center and the rear of the firearm and often (though not always) curved a little—almost like a little hook. The trigger almost always has solid band of metal or plastic surrounding and protecting it. This is called the *trigger guard*. It not only prevents the trigger from potentially being broken, it also protects against something (such as a shirt) accidentally snagging on the trigger and firing the gun unintentionally.

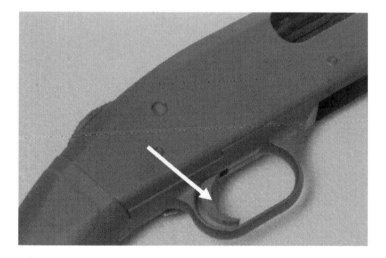

Figure 4 – The arrow points to the trigger of a shotgun

The trigger has a single purpose—to fire the gun. That is its only function. Therefore, unless you, or someone else, *intend* to fire the gun, there should not be a finger on, or near, the trigger for any reason.

Application of Knowledge: Gun Safety

Now you can explain the basics of how a gun works. You can also look at just about any gun in existence and identify a few critical parts. The two most important—parts you should remember even if you hate guns with a passion—are the muzzle and the trigger.

Muzzle comes first. The key here is maintaining awareness of two separate concepts that are of equal importance. The first is where the muzzle itself is pointed. The second is what direction is the *safest* alternative.

This is one area where this approach to gun safety differs a bit from what you may see in other places. I will discuss this more in the next chapter but, for now, please understand that there may not, in fact, be a "safe" place to point the muzzle of a gun in the real world, at least not as this would be defined on a shooting range. Consider the following illustration:

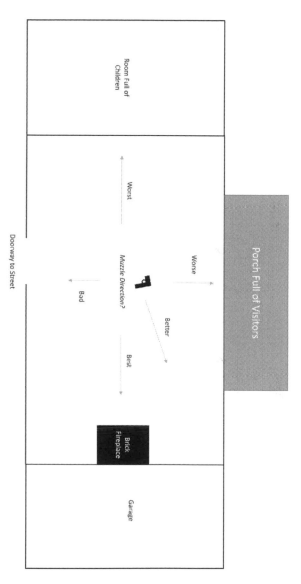

Figure 5 – Assume that you *must* handle a gun and point it
horizontally in this situation.
Where is the best place to point the muzzle?

In this situation, there is not a "perfect" answer. However, it is likely that a brick fireplace, backing up to an empty garage, would mitigate the harm from any live round being fired better than any of the other options.

What if, in this same scenario, there was suddenly a lethal threat, perhaps coming from the porch area? In this case, the porch might suddenly become the "safest" direction to point the muzzle. This would allow you to address the immediate threat to your (and perhaps your child's) life. Pointing a weapon in the direction of a crowd of people would never be acceptable on a commercial shooting range. However, it *might* be the best and only option available in this case.

These examples are intentionally extreme and abstract; however, hopefully they have effectively illustrated the point. In the real world there are no berms and there are no bullet traps. There is only the scenario that happens to exist around us at any given time. Muzzle control is, therefore, not as simple as it is on a range.

You cannot pick a single direction in which the muzzle will always be pointed and then stop thinking about it. Instead, you must be aware of both the direction of the muzzle and of the environment around you. Whenever you handle a gun, be sure that you are continuously aware of these two considerations and then *choose* to point the muzzle in the *safest* direction that you can. (Do not forget that up and down are both options!) Owning a gun is a thinking person's game.

Next comes the trigger. We have already seen that we should never touch the trigger unless we intend to fire the gun. Since we are discussing something that includes human actions and physical skills, however, it is also very helpful to have something specific *to do,* rather than simply a list of prohibitions.

Knowing what not to do is great, but it does not typically help you do things that solve problems. It is also likely to either cause you to freeze with inaction or to simply ignore what you know because you cannot figure out how to apply it. You know not to touch the trigger; however, this is of limited value when you need to pick up a gun and move it or use it.

Whenever you touch a gun, it is an appropriate and accepted practice to straighten the trigger finger and press it against the side of the gun — unless of course you intentionally place it on the trigger for the purposes of firing.

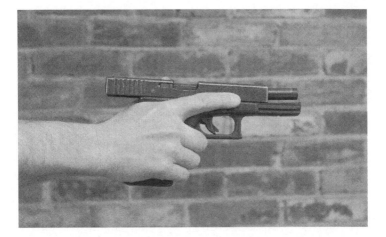

Figure 6

Figure 7 – The trigger finger should be straight and pressed against the side of the gun whenever it is not placed *purposefully* on the trigger

As you develop in your shooting skills, the general concept that you will want to apply is to associate the alignment of the sights of the gun on a target with the placement of your finger onto the trigger. There is more nuance involved in this, especially in tactical and defensive shooting. However, this basic concept will serve you well as you begin to develop in your skills.

In the interest of being thorough, and because of the potential life and death nature of gun safety, I believe that it is important to add a brief comment about mechanical failures here. *Most* modern firearms can take quite a beating, with a live round in the chamber, and nothing will happen (i.e., the gun will not fire) unless the trigger is pressed.

However, this is not *always* the case. There are some firearms that can impact fire (the gun will go off if it is impacted — without the trigger being pressed), including the very popular Remington 870 pump shotgun. (This is a fine gun. It is simply important to know that there is a chance it will fire if it is dropped with a round in the chamber). It is also true that even the best mechanical systems can fail sometimes, especially in extreme situations. It is never a good idea to depend completely on a mechanical system to prevent a gun from going off.

Always adhere to the basics of gun safety.

And with respect to safety fundamentals...that's it! Those are the fundamental components of gun safety. Muzzle awareness and trigger finger awareness are the key. Everything else is secondary.

Chapter Four:

Understanding Gun Safety Structures

Believe it or not, the gun industry is very good at safety — *on the shooting range*. Accidents on ranges do happen. However, they are relatively rare in formal, purpose-built infrastructure and training environments. Everyone generally accepts that guns are dangerous. Most people do not want to get hurt or to get somebody else hurt or killed. In most shooting range environments, there are many rules and, often, some sort of range safety officer to enforce them.

The problem is that shooting ranges are highly specialized environments — they are designed to contain real bullets being fired on purpose! A shooting range has at least one specified direction (usually called a berm or a bullet trap) in which bullets are supposed to be fired.

There is nothing wrong with this. It is the essence of what makes a shooting range useful. It is also completely different than almost any other environment in which a person can find himself or herself in modern society, as we saw in the previous Chapter.

Most places that the average person goes on a day-to-day basis, whether home, work, recreation, or simply transiting from place to place, do not have a direction that is designed and intended to support the firing of live rounds. Because of this fundamental difference, many of the habits and practices that are used very effectively for gun safety on shooting ranges are much less successful in other environments.

Shooting range safety practices are usually based around the *infrastructure* of the range—specifically the berm or bullet trap. When this infrastructure does not exist, these practices can become much less effective. Many people primarily handle guns within the confines of a shooting range; however, every gun owner also has moments when they will certainly handle a firearm off the range and away from the infrastructure that allows shooting ranges to operate safely.

It is typically in these moments (even if they only occur for cleaning, maintenance, storage, and transportation to or from the range) that safety issues occur. Any safety measure that only works well on a shooting range is, therefore, of limited practical value. This certainly is not to disparage range safety. Gun safety in any environment, range included, is critical. Nor is this to encourage you to ignore the rules that are in place at your local range — please do not!

Rather, my intent is to point out that your basis for and ability to safely handle a gun must not be based on the environment of the shooting range. If you own a gun, you must be able to handle it safely everywhere, not just in places that are designed to facilitate firing live rounds. Many of the range-focused safety structures (such as the four standard rules of firearms safety) that you will encounter simply are less than ideal for this purpose.

Consider the following anecdote: I have a friend, and former security co-worker, who spent more than two decades in the special operations community. This included more than a decade at one of the most elite military units in the world. He has been to virtually every high-level shooting school and tactical training program that there is. After leaving the military, he specialized in conducting high-threat security operations, mostly in active war zones. He has conducted well over forty operational deployments (*after* leaving the military) supporting the ongoing war on terror. My friend has been carrying guns professionally, at the pinnacle of the profession, for more than three decades.

Several years ago, he and I were discussing training and training methods when he mentioned that a few people that he knew in his local area had approached him. They were interested in some entry-level training.

He commented that he intended to refer them to me, which I questioned. After all, my friend is a better shooter than I am, with far more training and experience than I will ever have. His response was fascinating. "Yeah, but you know all that training stuff — like the four safety rules. I don't remember any of that," he told me.

How is this possible? How can a man who is, literally, one of the most skilled and experienced armed professionals in the world not know the four fundamental firearms safety rules? The answer has two parts. First, it is not what we know and can recite about guns and gun safety that keeps us safe with guns — *it is what we do with guns that matters.*

Without hesitation I would move down a hallway or through a door searching for unknown threats, in a war zone, while my friend, with a loaded gun in his hands, was behind me. In fact, I have. I never had even the slightest concern that he might have a gun safety mishap. There was frankly a much greater risk that I would do something unsafe in that environment than there was that he would.

Our respective levels of competency for safely handling firearms had nothing to do with being able to recite lists of rules. They had everything to do with each of our individual abilities to maintain awareness and control of both the muzzle of our weapon and the position of our trigger finger relative to what was going on around us. Only *what we actually did* with the guns in our hands mattered.

My friend does not need to remember a list of rules that do not often apply to what he does with guns in order to handle them safely, with extraordinary competence. While this is a bit over simplified (ignoring some tactical considerations and mechanical aspects of different weapons), he simply needs to be aware of his environment, aware of the muzzle, and to control the position of his trigger finger.

The second reason that my friend does not need to (and does not) remember the details of any of the standard firearms safety structures is that many of these various rule sets are either dependent on, or based around, the assumption that guns are being handled within the infrastructure of a shooting range. People who carry guns in the real world do not have this structure to rely on, therefore, much of this can often be irrelevant to real world needs.

Allow me to reiterate, for effect, that I am not encouraging you to ignore *any* firearm safety rules that an instructor, or a range facility may use. Quite the opposite. I strongly encourage you to *always* take the time to learn, and follow, the protocols that are in place.

Rules, protocols, and other types of gun safety structures are fundamentally what allow firing ranges and firearms competition to consistently be *very* safe environments. Many of these also are extremely good principles that, while they may not apply universally in the real world, are certainly worth consideration and virtually universal application, especially in training environments (more on this in Chapter 6).

As you learn more and develop in your gun-related knowledge and skills, you will undoubtedly be exposed to a wide variety of different concepts, theories, methods, and structures for firearms safety. The fundamental, and inviolable, rules of muzzle and trigger finger awareness and control do not supersede or replace these. They are simply the ground-level fundamentals that always apply, in every environment ranging from a well-lit gun shop to a running urban gun battle in the dead of night. They are the base upon which everything else is built.

CHAPTER FIVE:

GUN SAFETY WITH CHILDREN IN THE HOME

That what happens when you have a gun in your hand can be a literal matter of life and death obviously cannot be overstated. In the same manner, gun storage is also a critically important topic. This is particularly true for gun owners who have children, or who may have other people's children visit their home. In fact, this second case can often be of greater concern because other people's children may not have the knowledge, training, or experience that children who have been raised and mentored by responsible gun owners do.

I recommend applying a layered approach to firearms safety with children in the home. Depending on a single method for safety or security is rarely the most effective approach. It is better to have multiple points of failure that must occur before a tragedy can happen.

38

Please note that the following recommendations are not the "only way." They are not absolute rules, nor are they *all* necessarily appropriate or realistic to implement in every situation (though it is certainly worth striving to do so). However, following these principles will help you integrate gun ownership into your life safely. They will also allow you, if you so choose, to make your family safer in the effort by functionally integrating the self-defense capability of a firearm (or firearms).

Recommendation 1: Condition

If a gun is kept specifically for home defense and will not carried outside the home, I recommend that it be stored *without* a round in the chamber. This provides a barrier to a child making the firearm function, should they, in fact, gain access to it. This is also the preferred storage method by fire departments, as a gun with a round in the chamber is likely to go off, should it be caught in a house fire.

However, I do also recommend that a defensive handgun be carried on your person with a round in the chamber. I further recommend only using one firearm condition for any single defensive firearm or firearm type in use.

This is because of how we learn and apply skills. In a stressful setting, you are likely to respond in *exactly* the same way that you have trained and practiced. If you have only practiced with a round in the chamber, but store your self-defense weapon without one, then you are much less likely to succeed, should a self-defense situation occur.

If a single firearm (in this case almost certainly a handgun) is both carried concealed outside the home *and* actively used for defense inside the home (as opposed to being put into storage while another type of weapon, such as a shotgun, is relied upon for home defense), I do recommend that it always have a round in the chamber, whether it is being carried, or temporarily stored as a home-defense tool.

Recommendation 2: Mechanically controlled access

This concept is simple. If you want to prevent access to something, lock it up. However, in practice this becomes more complicated when a gun in the home is intended for self-defense purposes. Defense to an emergent threat such as a home invasion requires that responsible parties can access the gun quickly and efficiently under less-than-ideal conditions that can include haste, stress, and limited visibility.

There are several safes on the market that provide both some protection from unauthorized access and rapid accessibility to the firearm. For firearms that are intended for home defense, I generally recommend using one of these that does not require a physical key in order to retrieve the gun. I lean towards models that do not require battery power; however, this is a personal preference.

Firearms not intended for defensive employment can be stored in a safe that does not provide quick access. Large safes are expensive; however, many firearms have critical parts (such as barrels, bolt carriers, and trigger housing groups) that can easily be removed and placed in a small, relatively inexpensive safe. While this does not prevent theft of the entire firearm, it does render each firearm inoperable and secures the critical components without the need for a safe that is large enough to hold the gun, or guns. This can significantly reduce the cost associated with safely storing guns in a way that greatly mitigates the potential for accidents and misuse.

Recommendation 3: Height Controlled Access

This is certainly not a determinative protection; however, it does provide another barrier to, especially, a young child accessing a firearm—even if only a time delay that provides more of an opportunity for an adult to intervene before access occurs. Given the choice, firearms and quick-access safes for home defense that may provide less protection than a high-security safe, should be stored at chest level or above. This implements a layer of protection that limits the ability of small children to either find or attempt to access a gun.

Recommendation 4: Profile

The principle is simple. Visible firearms are more likely to be accessed by a curious child who does not live in the home. Curiosity and desire in general are not aroused without some sort of stimulus. Therefore, a gun (or gun safe) that people do not know is there is less likely to be accessed than one that is easily visible. This measure may also provide a measure of protection against theft, particularly from petty burglary.

Recommendation 5: Education

This measure is specifically related to gun owners who have children in, or who regularly visit, their homes. Children are naturally curious. Removing the mystery and *mentoring* them to be safe and responsible firearms users is one of the best barriers to tragedy. My 2017 book, *Mentoring Shooters: The Gun Owner's Guide to Building a Firearms Culture of Safety and Personal Responsibility* is specifically written as a guide to mentoring others, to include friends and family members.

CHAPTER SIX:

FURTHER SAFETY
RECOMMENDATIONS

If you have read this far, you should fully understand the fundamental requirements of gun safety and safe gun ownership. However, as I mentioned in Chapter Four, there are some additional concepts, often included within other models of gun safety, that can have much value in day-to-day administrative gun ownership, handling, and use.

The Building Shooters model for firearms safety also includes three recommendations. The difference between the two fundamental rules and the recommendations is that the rules *always* apply. The recommendations are things someone should train to do (and should do) but that may not apply in all situations.

Recommendation 1: Check the condition
of a gun each and every time it is handled.

This is really important. In fact, in terms of daily firearms safety, it is probably the most important thing that somebody can do aside from muzzle and trigger finger discipline. The only reason that I do not define this has a rule is because there are times when it might not be possible. In an administrative environment though, it should always happen. Checking the weapon costs nothing and can save everything.

An example of when this *would not* apply is if there is a lethal threat — making it so that your life is in danger. If you must draw your weapon to defend yourself, you are not going to take the time to verify whether your holstered weapon is loaded or not. In that situation, you can't. You are depending instead on the checks that you did *before-hand*.

Recommendation 2: Do not place a finger
on the trigger unless the sights are aligned on a target.

If you recall, I already mentioned this back in Chapter Three. The fact that trigger finger position makes it into both the rules *and* the recommendations should give you an indication of how important it is. Even though this is something that the firearms industry tends to ignore sometimes on shooting ranges, you should *never* ignore it.

The association that you want to develop is the combination of sight alignment and sight picture on the target with the finger being placed on the trigger. Eventually, this should become automatic. When the sights are not on a target, your finger should automatically come off the trigger. As the sights acquire the target and align, the finger should find the trigger – *if* the decision to fire has been made. The reason I do not define this as a rule is because there are times, such as close contact shooting situations during self-defense, where you might not have a traditional, visual sight picture when you press the trigger.

*Recommendation 3: Be sure of the target
and what is in front of and beyond it.*

Out in the real world, you are almost always going to be legally responsible and personally accountable for where the bullets go and what they hit. I am not just talking about self-defense situations either. In most cases, if you shot it, you bought it. This is also important on a shooting range, especially if the range is not designed for total containment.

For example, sometimes outdoor ranges are set up in

such a way that you can fire a round outside the range if you make a mistake. Maybe it is over the top of the berm or bullet trap, or maybe you can simply set your targets up in the wrong position and miss the backstop altogether. This book is not about range design; however, when you are on a firing range, you want *every* round to impact the bullet trap or backstop/berm, regardless of the position of the targets and shooters or direction of fire.

In an academic or administrative environment, being aware of all things relevant to the target is an easy thing to talk about. Even on a range, it is not necessarily always intuitively obvious, but neither is it rocket science. However, out in the real world, where situations and environments requiring self-defense are often fast, brutal, and dynamic, there tend to be a lot of unknown variables.

These types of situations are also generally not of the choosing of law-abiding citizens—meaning that the place and time that they happen is often outside of our control and the environments may be unfamiliar to us. In these types of scenarios, complete situational awareness and being aware of *everything* that could be relevant (like what is on the other side of a wall) may actually be impossible. This is one reason I do not define this as a rule. It is more of an idealized objective in the real world than it is an absolute rule that can realistically be adhered to.

The second reason I define this as a recommendation instead of a rule is that there are some situations for some armed professionals where this might not apply. These situations are not generally applicable for either civilian or law enforcement use in the United States; however, they do exist. In the Building Shooters safety model, if there are times when you might not do it, it cannot be defined as a rule.

You should now have a firm grasp of our firearms safety structure. There are two rules, five recommendations for storage, and three general recommendations for daily handling and use. These methods are not "the only way." However, if learned and applied, I believe that they are the most complete and effective structure for gun safety currently in existence. If you can understand and follow these basic principles, you are well on your way to becoming a safe and responsible gun owner.

SECTION II:
HOW YOUR BRAIN WORKS AND WHY IT MATTERS

Have a discussion with almost anyone about training and one of the things you will hear almost immediately is how people have different learning styles. The problem is, this actually isn't true....

CHAPTER SEVEN:

WHY THE BRAIN IS IMPORTANT

At Building Shooters, we have a very particular industry focus: application of brain and psychology research to training design. This may seem to be an odd area of focus for the firearms industry. However, during my time in the navy, when I saw military police officers who could not consistently grip a handgun after six weeks of firearms training, I realized how inefficient and ineffective our standard methods of training really are. This started me on the path to learn both why what we do does not work very well as well as how to fix it.

Over the two decades since then I have been focused on finding ways to improve the ways in which we develop fundamental levels of skill in, particularly, entry-level students. What I have learned during that time is that it is all about the brain!

Our brains are the control system for, and basis of,

everything that our bodies do, everything we think, everything we learn, and every decision that we make. They are also incredibly complex. As this book is being written in 2021, even the most advanced levels of modern science are just starting to possess the tools necessary to start attempting to unravel its mysteries.

Nevertheless, the information that we do have, and what is currently understood about how our brains function, is enough to make clear some harsh realities that I call the two fundamental failures of training. We fail in how we deliver training—standard training methods used in the firearms industry are misaligned with how the brain receives and retains information. We also fail in how we measure training success and performance—we have never had a method of exercising the same physiological and neurological systems that are needed during real-world use of a gun while measuring skill performance in ways that matter.

Hopefully, you noticed that both failures are related to how the human brain works. The brain's operation is the most important element of, literally, everything we do. Therefore, improving the outcome of anything we do must start with the brain. It is the fundamental infrastructure that everything else is built upon.

Correcting these two failures is the reason Building Shooters exists. Over the next several chapters I will explain, in layman's terms, how the brain is structured, how it learns, and what you need to know about how this will impact you as a new gun owner.

Chapter Eight:

The Brain as an Information System

This is the subject of my 2016 book, *Building Shooters*. If you want to learn more about this and see how it can be applied to improve training design and delivery methods for tactical applications, or if you want to see the scientific research behind this discussion, *Building Shooters* is the place to start. Here, I will merely provide a brief synopsis.

A Systems View

It is helpful to think of the brain, not as a biological organ, but as an information system. There are, in fact, many similarities between how the brain works and how advanced computing and information systems work.

The reason for this is that the human brain *is* an information system — the most advanced yet discovered in the universe. It is used as a model that drives much of the development in advanced information processing and high-performance computing.

What follows is a very simple model of the brain. It is not intended to be a biologically accurate depiction. It *is* intended to help you understand how our brains process and learn new information.

Input and Processing

All new information is received by one of the five senses. It is important to understand that the senses receive a massive amount of data. In fact, they receive so much that if people were aware of all of it, we would be unable to function effectively. To keep us from becoming overwhelmed, the brain has a filter. This prevents most of the information received by the senses from ever reaching the brain's processing and storage centers.

If information manages to get through the filter, it enters a space called short-term memory. You can think of this like the random-access memory (RAM) in a computer. It stores a small amount of information that can be worked with and used temporarily. However, it does not retain anything for long periods of time.

Storage

If information is going to be stored, it first must be *physically moved* from the short-term system and placed into one, or both, of two long-term memory storage systems. This process is not automatic. It also does not happen instantly.

Current models of the brain contain three memory systems. *Short-term memory,* described above, is very small when compared to the rest of the brain's storage and processing capacity. Long-term *declarative memory* is a very large storage system, of virtually infinite storage capacity. Declarative memory is marked by the storage of consciously accessed information. The third system is called long-term *procedural memory.* The procedural system is also very large, with virtually infinite storage capacity. However, unlike declarative memory, the procedural system is marked by *unconscious* access.

Both the long-term memory systems, procedural and declarative, can store the same information. However, they are each located in different geographic regions of the brain and are therefore considered to be functionally separate systems. The information storage between them can often be redundant. However, how, and when, the information in each system is accessed and used is different. As you will see, this is of particular interest to gun owners who are interested in self-defense.

The Role of Procedural Memory

One of the unique aspects of the long-term procedural memory system is that it is the only memory system that can be reliably accessed when a person is under stress. This means that, if we hope to be able to perform a skill during a self-defense situation, it is not enough to understand, do, practice, or even to learn and be able to perform a skill very effectively. For self-defense use, the skill *must* also be stored within the procedural memory system. If it is not, it is unlikely that you will be able to access and apply it during a self-defense situation.

As you can see, understanding the brain, and how it works, is an incredibly important part of effectively learning to use a gun, especially if part of your goal is self-defense. In the next Chapter we will look at how the brain learns, and how you can use this knowledge to your advantage as you begin the process of learning gun-related knowledge and skills.

CHAPTER NINE:

THE LEARNING PROCESS

If you are reading this book, it is a virtual certainty that you are familiar with several different models and methods of education and teaching. You are also familiar with learning. After all, you learned to read, and somebody probably taught you how!

Teaching vs. Learning

Teaching and learning are often considered to be the same thing in discussions. However, this simply is not true. All of us have sat through a training event, such as a week-long work seminar, where we may have attended forty hours of training, but we certainly did not learn forty hours-worth of information!

Most of us have also done some sort of online learning (often compliance training for work) where we have spent hours clicking through slides packed with information that we could not hope to recall with any level of detail. It is perfectly possible to teach without learning. In fact, it is more than possible. It is common!

A significant amount of the common-use educational methods (and not just in firearms training!) are designed around teaching efficiency rather than learning efficiency. Teaching and course materials make the information available to the student, but *learning* the material is something the student must often do on their own time.

The Unique Aspects of Gun-Related Training

Learning to use a gun is, unique — and not just because of the, often, controversial nature of the subject matter. There are several specific aspects to gun training that make it fundamentally different that most other subjects that you will ever learn about. This is especially true if you are interested in using a gun for self-defense purposes.

The first of these unique aspects is the fact that self-defense situations *only* happen when the human body is experiencing a tremendous amount of stress. In fact, this is pretty much a pre-requisite for self-defense in general. During self-defense with a gun, it is almost always a legal prerequisite for you to be in imminent danger of death or serious bodily harm before the gun can be used. A very high amount of stress is pretty much guaranteed.

As we learned in the previous Chapter, this means that it is not enough for us to simply learn about guns, or to learn gun skills. If we want to have the ability to use a gun for self-defense, it is also critical that we learn in such a way that the information and skills are stored in our *procedural memory system*.

The second thing that makes gun training unique is that both the subject matter and often the tool (gun) itself can make people extremely nervous. As an instructor, it is not unusual to see adult students, both men and women, who start visibly shaking when they first touch, even an unloaded gun inside a classroom.

There are probably a variety of reasons that this occurs, but from the perspective of learning, this means that it is often very difficult for people to learn anything during their initial exposure and training. This is simply because of the stress they are experiencing. Our brains do not learn very well when they are highly stressed.

The third thing that makes gun training unique is that the skills involved are highly progressive in nature. This application of the term progressive has nothing to do with modern politics. Rather it describes the fact that one skill, such as the ability to grip a handgun correctly, is required before other, more complex, skills such as presenting the gun towards a target and firing it can occur.

Gun skills, especially the core fundamentals of grip, aiming, trigger management, and various methods of presentation, stack on top of each other in a very progressive manner. If the core skills are not learned correctly, it will not be possible to learn to do anything else well when the technique in question is built upon poorly developed progressive subskills.

Learning How to Learn

As you start your journey into gun ownership and shooting, you will find that you have many choices with respect to methods of shooting, types of training, and different instructors. We will discuss these topics in the next section of this book. Here, what I want to ensure you understand is that *how* you are presented information and *how* you practice, particularly during your first few exposures to the tools and skills, can have long-lasting impacts on your development as a gun owner and shooter. The how, frankly, is just as important as the what.

Because of how the brain works, if you try to do too much too fast, or if you attend training programs that emphasize "cool experience" and "round count" over effective learning, you are likely to experience what are ultimately unnecessary setbacks and impediments to your skill development. Let me encourage you now to *take your time* in the beginning.

Learn the fundamentals—starting with rock-solid, safe administrative gun handling procedures—before moving on to more advanced skills. After you have learned something, it is much, much harder to unlearn it and replace it with something different than it is to simply learn the correct thing the first time around.

Consider the following graphic. It illustrates, conceptually, how information is typically presented to students during industry-standard firearms training courses, compared to the average student's actual skill retention and performance. In most cases, the bulk of the information is presented in a very short time period—with the student struggling to keep up. Eventually, the student's inability to learn the core fundamentals in such a compressed period limits his or her ability to continue advancing in skill performance. As fatigue sets in towards the end of the training period, the student's performance starts to degrade even farther.

In the weeks that follow, the student may be motivated enough to practice a bit, leading to a temporary pause in the degradation of their skills. Often, however, the same types of resources and facilities that were used in training will not be available to them outside the confines of formal instruction. As a result, particularly if the student fails to train religiously, their skill performance rapidly extinguishes to near zero. In fact, studies have shown that the aggregate skill level of a police officer in basic marksmanship, after academy training ends, is hardly better than that of that of an untrained person who has never even touched a gun before.

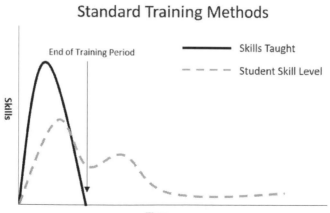

Figure 8 – The results of standard firearms training methods

Several years ago, I attended a course with a local instructor to gain some education credits towards maintaining an instructor certification. Of the people in the course, all had attended prior firearms training. Every person in the class had a permit to carry a handgun. Several of the students had attended "advanced" training programs with reputable and experienced local instructors within just a few months of attending this class. Yet, at the beginning of the course, I was still the *only* student who was unable to load and unload my pistol without instructor assistance—using dummy (inert) training rounds in a classroom.

It is tempting, when we encounter experiences such as this, to look for a person to blame. After all, it seems ridiculous. Surely it seems that there must be something wrong with either the student or the instructor when retention of something so seemingly basic is so poor. Hopefully, after reading to this point in this book, you now know better.

The fact of the matter is that the way we teach (and have always taught) these skills is largely ineffective when it comes to producing long-term learning. There is a better way and before you start your journey to becoming a gun owner and shooter, I want to show you both what it is and how to pursue it.

The Brain-Based Learning Process

In the second volume of my *On Training* book series, there is a section in which I debunk several common training myths that have long existed in the firearms industry. One of these is the idea that everyone has his or her own learning style that must be followed for a student to learn effectively. You may have heard this one yourself, even related to different topics. The trouble is that it simply is not true.

Healthy human brains all fundamentally learn the same way, using the same basic neurological processes. Not everyone necessarily starts a training program with the same pre-existing level of skills and knowledge — meaning everyone may have a different brain map when the course starts. However, the *ways* in which we learn are largely consistent from person to person.

Understanding this allows instructors to design and deliver training in ways that match how student's brains learn, at a neurological level. For you, understanding this will help you establish realistic expectations of learning and performance. It will also help to shape your training and practice efforts in ways that can maximize efficiency and effectiveness.

The details and scientific support, once again, are

contained in my book *Building Shooters*. For our purposes here, simply consider the following. When a skill, or piece of information, is first introduced, our brains are unlikely to even receive most of the information presented. This is because most of it is likely to be blocked by the "filter" that we discussed in Chapter 8.

This keeps our brains from becoming overwhelmed. It also makes it difficult for us to learn anything the first time that we are exposed to it. To address this fundamental reality of brain function, the first step in the learning process is to *prime* a new skill or piece of information. This means that it should be presented to the student, and practiced, without any expectation that the student learns or retains it.

It is important, of course, for instructors to understand this. It is also important for you, as a student, to do so. Expectation management of your own performance is an important component of learning. If you cannot remember something, or do something well, after the first time it is taught to you, do not feel like a failure. Do not assume there is something wrong with you. There is not! This simply means that you are a human being with a normally functioning brain. In fact, it would be incredibly unusual for you to learn something that is truly new the first time that it is presented to you.

After a skill, or piece of information, has been primed, it is typically important for there to be at least a twenty-four-hour period before it is *taught*—presented again in a detailed manner and practiced. The second time that you see the skill or information, you can now expect that your brain will recognize that it has seen it before and therefore let it pass through the "filter," into the short-term memory system.

This is a point where there is an opportunity to either help yourself, or an opportunity to screw things up. Recall from the last chapter that before information can be stored for the long-term, it first must be physically moved out of short-term memory and placed into at least one of the long-term memory storage systems.

This is not an instantaneous process. It takes time. It requires chemical processes to occur in the brain. It also requires that you *sleep* before it can be completed. If you feel like you are getting the fundamentals down, and then push for too much in a one-day period, you run the risk of corrupting the information and making it much more difficult (and more time consuming) to learn correctly.

A good example of this is the common training

practice of learning to grip a handgun, then moving on to learning to draw from the holster, all in the same day. What often happens is that, as you practice drawing from the holster, you will start to perform the grip with significant technical variations—because this skill has not yet been moved into long-term memory.

This practice can literally corrupt the (correct) method of skill performance that has been learned and act to *prevent* you from learning to grip a gun effectively. It certainly will make the process much more difficult and time consuming that it needs to be. A better approach is to learn and practice the grip correctly. Then, take between a twenty-four to forty-eight-hour break before the next lesson or training session begins. This "downtime" allows your brain to transfer the correctly learned information into long-term memory and frees up your short-term memory space to receive something new.

After the information or skill has been primed, then (after a twenty-four to forty-eight-hour break), taught, *then* given another twenty-four to forty-eight hours to be transferred into long-term memory, you should have now effectively *learned* a skill. However, you are not done. If you want to be good at the skill, and especially if you want to be able to use the skill for self-defense, then more is needed.

The next phase of learning, where something stored in long-term memory is both tweaked to improve performance and placed into the procedural (unconscious access) memory system so that it will be used under stress is called *enhancement*. There are many different methods and techniques that are used to enhance existing skills. However, for the purposes of this book, simply consider that skills, even those that are stored in long-term memory, are perishable. If we do not practice, our ability to perform degrades over time.

Similarly, if we only practice skills in isolation, and we never connect them during training to the other skills and thinking processes that are necessary for self-defense such as evaluating potential threats, moving, and making decisions, then our ability to apply them in the real world will be limited. This is true regardless of how good we may become at performing them in an isolated environment.

Consider the graphic below. It demonstrates how a brain-based approach to both teaching and learning skills works. Unlike the industry-standard approach, where massive amounts of information — far beyond the capacity of any student to learn—are presented in a short time period, the basic building blocks and skills are presented, and learned, relatively slowly.

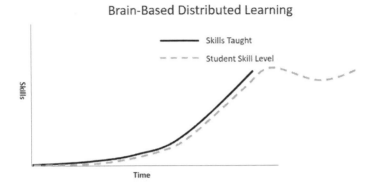

Figure 9 – The results of brain-based training methods

This teaching and learning should follow the process of *prime, teach, enhance* for each skill or piece of knowledge presented. As you learn the core fundamentals of gun handling and shooting, consolidate them into long-term memory, and then both improve them and connect them together through continued enhancement, you will find that your skills and knowledge will soon be capable of a near exponential rate of improvement, should you desire to pursue more advanced abilities.

Compare this to the earlier graph, which

demonstrates the effects that normally result from the industry-standard approaches to training. The *way* in which you approach learning can make a big difference, both in the results and in the efficiency of your efforts! A slower approach at the beginning will produce much faster results at the end. With a brain-based approach, you will not need to unlearn and then relearn incorrect, ineffective performance of fundamentals that are progressive components of more advanced shooting skills.

Understand that the difference in outcomes is not necessarily related to *what* is being taught to you. Rather, the difference is produced by *how* you approach learning it. Two different ways of learning the exact same material will produce markedly different results. As you pursue the development of gun-related knowledge and skill, I highly encourage you to consider how your brain works and use this knowledge to help structure your exposure to, and involvement in, various types of training and experiences.

Gun ownership and participation in the shooting sports and tactical training community can be very rewarding. There are a lot of fantastic people. There is a lot out there to be learned. There is a lot of fun to be had.

There are a lot of things to experience. It is important that you also understand that how you approach doing so, especially at the beginning, can make a big difference in your ultimate skill level and capability. It really is all about the brain!

CHAPTER TEN:

THE FALSE CHOICE

In this final chapter on learning, I want to briefly address something that you will probably encounter as you venture out into the firearms training world. Specifically, this is the idea that learning to use a gun effectively, especially for self-defense purposes, is an all or nothing proposition.

In some parts of the industry there is an almost-spoken assumption that you must either be a die-hard enthusiast, or simply give up and pack it in now. This is false. It is also detrimental not only to you, but to the industry. I want to explain why here, lest you encounter this attitude and be put-off enough to give up on the whole thing altogether.

In 2015, I wrote a small segment in former Marine, former police officer, and World-Champion competitive shooter Michael Seeklander's book *The Art of Instruction*.

The piece discusses the four primary elements that influence the firearms and tactical training industry. These are competitive shooters, vendors, elite units from military and law enforcement agencies, and liability.

Just looking at these influences by label, it is easy to see that most of the people involved in them either place their lives on the line daily in the top echelon of the armed professions, shoot competitively as a hobby and/ or profession, or make their living selling goods and services in the industry. In short, most of the people who influence the industry live it and breathe it on a daily basis.

This can sometimes create something of a one-sided view — one that does not always benefit people who may not share the same professional or personal interests. Yet, many people outside the industry, who may not be interested in entering "gun culture" per se, still recognize the benefits of and are interested in pursuing the personal capability that guns can provide to them.

To be fair, it is absolutely true that the more you practice (correctly!), the better you will be. It is also true that the more interest you have and the more focused and intent-oriented you are during your learning efforts and training, the better your results will be. While outside the scope of this book, these are also important aspects of how the brain learns. What is *not* true is the idea that becoming a safe, competent, and capable gun owner who has successfully integrated gun ownership into your life must become an all-encompassing lifestyle choice.

It certainly *can* become a lifestyle, and there is nothing wrong with this. Particularly if you desire to become a successful competitive shooter, there is no substitute for dedication and practice. However, you do not need to dedicate the rest of your life to combative shooting in order to attain, and maintain, a functional level of safety and self-defense skill. There *will* be some effort involved, but it need not be an all or nothing proposition.

This, in fact, is one of the main benefits to firearms and the inherent capability they provide. As the classic saying about Colonel Samuel Colt's popular "Peacemaker" revolver goes, *God made men, Sam Colt made them equal.* The tool itself provides the capability for individual physical equality in a way that nothing else can.

You should not take away from this discussion the idea that you can simply buy a gun, shoot it once (or take a one-day class) and deem yourself "ready" for whatever may come (or, frankly, even deem yourself ready to safely handle it). You *should* take away the idea that integrating a firearm into your life safely and adequately will require some up-front investment of time and effort. It need not be prohibitive, but some investment will be required.

Similarly, maintaining an adequate level of skill over the course of your life will require some ongoing maintenance and practice. This is no different than any other skill ranging from riding a bike, golfing, and driving a car, to typing or conducting mathematical calculations.

What is definitely *not* required is a deep affinity for guns or a burning desire to live and breathe gun culture, tactical training, or competitive shooting. A reasonable up-front time investment and some purpose-driven practice on a periodic basis are perfectly capable of developing and maintaining a very safe, very capable armed citizen.

SECTION III:
TRAINING

Whatever your intent with guns, be it
sporting use, recreation, self-defense,
competition, or some combination of
these, you must recognize and respect
that you are choosing to own and use
a tool that provides you tremendous
personal capability — including the
ability to kill or severely injure other
people with very little physical effort...

CHAPTER ELEVEN:

UNDERSTANDING COMMON TRAINING STRUCTURES

At the end of the previous chapter, we discussed in general terms the "armed lifestyle" and the false "all or nothing" choice that the commercial side of the firearms industry can sometimes present to curious or aspiring new shooters. Again, there is nothing wrong with any level of interest, nor with striving to attain any level of skill or capability in the various shooting disciplines. However, this presentation unfortunately can sometimes serve as a barrier that discourages people from accessing the freedom and equality that is available to them through the right to keep and bear personal arms.

Whenever I discuss these subjects with a prospective new gun owner, I always encourage them to invest the time to attain a reasonable level of knowledge and skill *first*, then consider the rest. If possible (depending on your local laws, this may or may not be possible), I often encourage people to learn the skills—even before they buy anything. This can lead to far better choices and more efficient use of funds when buying equipment.

You have probably noticed that I keep using a specific term when I talk about training and learning— that is *invest*. The use of this term is intentional, as that is exactly what training is. It is an investment.

Whatever your (legal) intent with guns, be it sporting use, recreation, self-defense, competition, or some combination of these, you must recognize and respect that you are choosing to own and use a tool that provides you tremendous personal capability— including the ability to kill or severely injure other people with very little physical effort. This capability can bring you tremendous benefits, including near peer-to-peer physical equality with any other human being. It also makes the tool itself inherently dangerous, which is why the first section of this book is entirely devoted to safety.

When you take the time to learn and train, you are quite literally investing in your own future and the future of those around you. You are investing time, and perhaps financial resources, just like you are putting a deposit into an investment account. In fact, you *are* putting a deposit into an investment account—just not a financial one. Just like a bank account, the more that you put into this investment, the more that will be available when you need to make a withdrawal.

The subject matter that we are directly talking about here is training. As a new participant in the industry, you will see that there are a variety of training options available to you. In the remainder of this chapter, I want to take a brief look at these options and discuss some of the things you should consider when you are looking to "invest" in your knowledge, skills and abilities.

Option One: One-Day Classes

In the civilian world, one-day classes are the primary basis of the training infrastructure, as it exists today. This is especially true at the local level. Many of these are the mandated "carry permit" courses. However, this type of program's acceptance as an appropriate training structure has produced a variety of spinoffs. Many instructors offer one-day courses in several different skills and disciplines. These are generally offered in local marketplaces with significant commercial success.

Why are one day classes the most common? First,

these courses are what people expect to see. This makes it easier to fill them. Sometimes (such as for permit classes) the structure of the classes can be mandated by regulation. A single day also represents a limited, finite investment for the student. Relatively speaking, it is easy to schedule a day to do something.

From the aspect of training (not learning), there are also some benefits to one-day classes. They are efficient from the perspective of just putting out information. They are not too short, where, by the time an instructor learns everybody's names, the students are walking out the door. There is also enough time to tailor some information and skills to match a student's specific needs.

Unfortunately, from a *learning* perspective, one-day programs are not an effective method of producing positive long-term results, *especially* for beginners. Over the course of a full day, far more information is typically presented than you will be capable of learning. What is taught and practiced tends to become corrupted. Poor technique development and poor retention are common byproducts of one-day courses for entry-level students.

Depending on your goals and your local area, you may well have little else than a one-day program to attend. The challenges that the format can present to your learning should not prevent you from seeking training. You should, however, be aware of these challenges and seek to mitigate them to improve your own learning value within the class's limitations.

Option Two: Half-Day Classes

Half-day classes have started becoming more and more common in the industry over the past ten years. On the learning side, half-day programs are better (or, more accurately, *can be* better) than one-day programs. They provide less time for the instructor to teach. Therefore, less is often taught, which can reduce the potential for neural interference during information storage.

When multiple, half-day sessions are used, the increase in learning potential for half-day programs really can provide tangible benefits. This format has the potential to take advantage of the capabilities of priming. It also facilitates the potential for effective consolidation to long-term memory.

Option Three: Multi-Day Classes

Multi-day classes (2–5 days, normally) are some of the most common "advanced" programs in the firearms industry. In terms of the market, multi-day classes are the ones that tend to cater to the systemic motivations of those students who look beyond the regulatory requirement.

From a *training* perspective, multi-day programs are great. Instructors have time to get to know the students. There is plenty opportunity to put out a great volume of knowledge and information and to customize the instruction to individual students. In terms of learning, however, multi-day programs are unfortunately difficult environments within which to develop long-term learning, especially (again) for beginning students.

The reason that these programs are not terribly effective for beginners is because there is no time for the structured *priming, teaching, enhancement* process that is required, neurologically, to produce long-term learning. Most of the skill performance ends up being done from the short-term memory system. As a result, significant effects of interference are often blatantly visible as the training progresses. Bad habits, ones that are very difficult to unlearn, can easily be picked-up in these types of environments by entry-level students, especially when stress is induced.

Option Four: Martial Arts Model

If you stop and think about it, treating firearms training like a martial art makes a lot of sense from both a subject matter and a learning perspective. Classes can be short (an hour or so). The information can be layered to exactly fit the student's level of skill and knowledge. Students only progress to the next level of training once they have actually *learned* the material from their current level. This is how the brain learns; therefore, a training system delivered this way can work quite well.

In terms of learning value, this sort of structure has no equal aside from perhaps private instruction (though this is arguable). Unfortunately, this does not currently meet the market's expectations for firearms training in most areas. Therefore, training programs structured in this way can sometimes be difficult to find.

Option Five: Personal Trainer

The concept of personal training needs no real explanation. It is a common structure for plenty of other industries, such as exercise and fitness. In the absence of other options, this type of structure should be what serious students, or entry-level students who want to learn efficiently and avoid developing bad habits that will be very difficult to unlearn, are looking for.

Training for a fight (including a gunfight) is not something you want to do for one to five days, then call it good. Even after the skills have been learned at a relatively high level, continuous practice, tactical application, etc. are necessary if you want to optimize the chances of real-world combative success.

Option Six: "PADI" Model

Another option is what I call the "PADI Model." PADI, as you may know already, is the professional association of dive instructors for SCUBA diving. Other types of programs (like Emergency Medical Technician training) also use this structure. One of the course formats is a series of evening or weekend classes that extends over a period of weeks to comprise a complete course. For example, a course could consist of classes two nights per week for six weeks.

This is a decent way to learn if the course is designed with brain function in mind. In fact, this models closely how I have structured developmental firearms training programs in the past, with excellent student success. I have personally delivered a significant amount of training this way and it is quite effective.

Unfortunately, this is another structure that is not common in the firearms market, partly because of the time-slot commitments required from both students and instructors. If you can find this in your local market it can be a good way to learn; however, it is not commonly available in most areas.

Option Seven: Online and Hybrid Training

In recent years, and especially in the wake of the COVID-19 pandemic, modern technology has introduced new methods and tools for training. The use of high-speed internet connections to make the transfer of information less location dependent with far greater scalability has opened new opportunities — and new risks — for firearms training.

The pandemic of 2020 pushed remotely delivered training into new prevalence. Now even some of the world's best instructors are delivering what used to be in-person training using a remote format. There are several ways this can be approached. Some of them are highly effective. Some of them are completely worthless. Ultimately, it is no different than any other method of training. To determine whether training is likely to be efficient and effective or not, *consider its impact on the brain*.

Is the training method introducing information with a *prime, teach, enhance* model — spread over time to allow transfer between memory systems and long-term retention? If so, then it is probably effective. If not, then it probably fails to produce long-term learning. The human brain is the constant in this equation. Keep its core functions in mind, and you will be able to accurately predict what training will be effective and what will not.

Four vendors who I am personally aware of that offer this type of training (and online information) that is at least nominally structured for learning are: Mike Seeklander at www.shooting-performance.com; Defensive Mindset Training in Minneapolis at www.defensivemindsettraining.com; Distributed Security, Inc. at www.distributedsecurity.com; and Mike "Ox" at www.dryfiretrainingcards.com.

By way of full disclosure, I know these vendors personally and was also previously the director of training for the original entity (Sealed Mindset) that eventually became Defensive Mindset Training. You will see quotes from several of them on some of my book covers. I receive no royalties or proceeds from their training businesses. By all accounts, many of the results from their remote, hybrid, and online programs are exceptional.

Each of these sources (like anything else) surely has its own capabilities and limitations. Training sources are also not exclusive. Variety is the spice of life (when it is not corrupting your skills at least) and you will doubtless find much continuity between the information offered between them.

It goes without saying that multi-time World Champion Mike Seeklander is far and away the best technical shooter in this group. With respect to tactics, the folks at Distributed Security have one of (if not the) most complete training programs ever made available to civilians. They also have a specific entry level program for new gun owners that you can peruse at www.firstgunowners.com.

Summary: Application

Depending on the local training options available to you, and personal resources you have available, it is possible for you to be limited to attending in-person training that is formatted into suboptimal learning structures. This will almost certainly be true with regulatory and mandatory training such as permit to carry classes. If you find yourself in this situation, do not be discouraged! You can still have a great impact on your own learning destiny.

Consider focusing on the most fundamental skill in the class—one that is a building block to other, more complex skills, skill sequences, or applications—and dedicating yourself to doing that skill correctly. If the class begins to outpace your ability to perform correctly, slow down, calm down, and do that one skill right. Do not worry too much about learning everything being taught in the class. Focus on being safe and learning that building block skill correctly.

If you learn it well, you can learn the rest later. If you do not, learning the rest will be far more difficult. Consider asking the instructor to help you modify a drill or exercise for the purpose of honing the area you are working on. Even consider asking the instructor to help you identify the specific thing you should focus on.

I want to make clear that I am not advising you under any circumstances to ignore the instructor's direction or drills in a class and simply do your own thing instead. This (legitimately) will make instructors uneasy, as it makes you unpredictable and seemingly unwilling or unable to follow instructions. Ignoring an instructor may well get you kicked off a range or out of a class— justifiably so.

Understand that while firearms training is generally a very safe activity, every live-fire training environment is still fundamentally only one trigger press away from a fatality. Ensuring a safe training environment means that instructors need to be able to control what happens on the range. This requires understanding what students will do, and when.

In many cases, a short conversation prior to a class with the instructor about personal goals, personal skill status, and objectives can be very appropriate. If you tell an instructor that you need to work on a specific skill, such as grip, and possibly even that you intend to come back and repeatedly re-take the same class from that instructor—so you can master the rest of the skills involved—most instructors will be onboard. This discussion may also help you determine if the class you want to take is appropriate for you, *at that time*.

If an instructor is unfamiliar with brain-based learning, feel free to show them this book, or refer them to our website at www.buildingshooters.com. I will be more than happy to correspond with, and provide free access to any of my books, to any instructor who contacts me on behalf of a student to learn more about brain-based training methods and design. Changing the industry for the better has always been my primary objective.

While there is disagreement on many things in the industry, one thing almost every instructor has in common is that we all want the best for our students. Everyone in the industry also wants a safe range. If any instructor does not, walk away.

CHAPTER TWELVE:

CHOOSING AN INSTRUCTOR

The previous chapter focused on some of the different types of training structures you will find, along with some considerations that go along with each of them. The bottom line is that some training, even excellent training from superb instructors, may not be appropriate for an entry-level student. If you try to do too much too fast it can make the road to skill development much longer and more arduous than it needs to be.

You can, of course, influence this a great deal yourself. However, the instructor and the structure of the course are also extremely important influences. The right instructor, with the right curriculum, at the right time, can make all the difference in the world. The wrong instructor (or even a great instructor at the wrong time) can sometimes do more lasting harm than good.

In this chapter, I want to take a little time to discuss

choosing an instructor, including a few characteristics to look for and evaluate. That an instructor should understand, practice, and enforce safety goes without saying, but it still bears repeating. Safety comes first.

It is worth noting here that safety does not necessarily look like a long list of rigid rules and a "boot camp" mentality. Recall the first section of this book about firearms safety and the story of my friend, an extraordinarily skilled shooter and highly experienced armed professional who does not bother trying to remember any standard list of "rules." Safety is not about what we write, say, or preach, it is about what we actually *do* with guns. Muzzle and trigger finger awareness — always.

Characteristic 1: Instructor Experience and Training

This may seem an odd characteristic to list first; however, it may be one of the most important, especially for a new student. It is tempting to look for the longest list of tactical accolades and schools — certainly these make good marketing collateral!   Indeed, it is certainly true that an instructor must be competent. An instructor must know well, and be proficient at, the material that they are teaching you. It is difficult to impart knowledge to a student that you do not have. However, it is also true that the instructor's primary role is not to perform shooting skills or tactics in front of you; it is to *enable you to learn* those same skills.

A highly experienced and proficient tactical operator, law enforcement officer, or competitive shooter may, in fact, be a wonderful instructor. Then again, they may not be. Many military and law enforcement personnel *do* take formal instructor training or fill formal instructor roles. However, this is not necessarily a part of these jobs.

Many armed professionals are also vastly undertrained with respect to the "armed" part of the job. Understand that working (or having worked) as an armed professional makes a person neither knowledgeable about shooting, nor good at teaching it.

Lest there be confusion, I am by no means suggesting that you should simply find the person who has taught the largest volume of classes. Often these programs are bulk, "cattle call" environments with classrooms full of students who may learn next to nothing at all. If your objective is to learn, this is not what you want.

I also am not suggesting that the instructor's skill and knowledge do not matter. They do indeed matter. An instructor who is not skilled enough to understand the correct performance of the fundamentals of shooting will certainly not be able to pass them on to you.

What I am suggesting is that you should also consider an instructor's experience with teaching, and more importantly, *ability as an instructor*. This should be a primary consideration in your evaluation process.

This is particularly true during your first few entry-level lessons, as you learn the fundamentals of gun handling and basic shooting mechanics. You need someone skilled enough to teach you correctly. You also need someone who understands that his or her main job is not to tell you things, yell at you, or show off, *it is to help you learn.*

Characteristic 2: Demeanor

There are a variety of different styles of instruction. It is the same with range management and I want to be careful here. Virtually all people (certainly I am in this category) have idiosyncrasies that, if taken to extremes, would be detrimental to their ability as an instructor. Furthermore, there is almost always more than one way to "skin the cat." I do not intend to impugn anyone with this section of the book. I do, however, want to lay out a few patterns that I have observed over the years in the hopes that they will be helpful to you as you look for instructors to help teach and guide you.

First, while there can often be value in a "command presence" on, especially, a live fire range, any instructor who runs a range like he or she is running a boot camp is, at best, failing to create an effective learning environment. This can sometimes add value (though still not for student learning) in professional settings, such as the military. However, running a "by the numbers" boot-camp style experience in civilian classes generally tends to mean that the instructor has little of value to teach, knows this (at least at some level), and therefore compensates for it by being rigidly controlling—and often extremely loud.

Characteristic Three: Resume Building

Another potential trait to watch out for is an instructor who frequently, and excessively, attempts to build themselves up in front of the class. This usually happens through an exhaustive rehearsal of the instructor's resume (usually including a laundry list of what famous schools they have attended and what famous people in the community they know etc.). Often this is then followed by endless stories of heroics and such.

Now, to be fair, it is not unusual for an instructor to introduce themselves and explain their background. In fact, it would be abnormal for this not to happen in a class. It can also be appropriate for an instructor to share a personal story that relates to a topic being taught in the class.

I also must advise granting a bit of leeway, especially in marketing materials, for people who make their living as instructors. When you must pay the bills, you must find a way to drive revenue. However, if an instructor spends most of their time telling you about themselves and trying to impress you with how cool they are, this typically is not a positive indicator.

It is a simple fact that you cannot hide on a range. Neither timers nor targets lie. You hit or you miss. People who can actually shoot will usually tend to talk much less about how good of a shooter they are than people who are not as confident in their ability.

Remember that an instructor has limited time with you and their job should be to *help you learn*. If an instructor has much hard-earned knowledge to share, they will usually share it with you. That is why you are paying them. If they do not, some may compensate by sharing never-ending stories about how much knowledge they have—without ever seeming to reveal any.

Characteristic Four: Appearance

One other thing that is worth considering is how an instructor physically presents to the students. Of course, different classes will have different attire and equipment requirements, so calibrate this accordingly. It is neither unusual, nor inappropriate, for people (instructors and students both) to wear some sort of range attire, including hats, cargo or tactical pants, and specialized belts. Often ranges or formal programs will even have some sort of uniform for instructors. This is all fine and normal.

However, in my personal experience it also tends to be a consistent principle that a person's skill and knowledge is inversely proportional to their level of "tact-i-cool" clothing and gear. This rule tends to apply most accurately when tactical clothing and gear are voluntarily, and obnoxiously, worn in environments where they add no specialized value.

Some folks just really like gear—and good on 'em. Nothing wrong with that. They are keeping the vendors employed! However, sometimes this can also be an effort to gain respect, or status, that is fundamentally rooted in insecurity—and this not necessarily a positive indicator of an instructor's knowledge or skill.

In all cases, remember that safety comes first and that an instructor's job is not to impress you, or even to entertain you, but rather to help you learn. Aside from safety, your learning is really the only metric that truly matters.

CHAPTER THIRTEEN:

PRIORITIZING

There are generally two main segments of the shooting skill development timeline. The first is initial training and learning. This is where you go from zero to wherever your baseline skill level is. What this looks like, of course, can differ greatly from person to person.

If you want to be a competitor, or if you become a highly skilled recreational or defensive shooter, this period may never really end. If this describes you, then you can look forward to many challenging, enjoyable, (often frustrating!), and highly rewarding years ahead of you as you learn, refine, learn again, and chase perfection in whatever discipline(s) you choose.

However, not everyone who owns a gun falls into this category and, as I have said previously, this is OK!

There are many people who do not want to dedicate their life to attaining an elite level of skill yet who still recognize and value the capability that safe, competent firearms use can provide to them and their families. If you fall into this second category, then this chapter is for you!

If you are a real person with family, competing interests, other hobbies, and limited resources (both financial and otherwise), then you know that, in most cases, something must give. You do not have, and will not have, unlimited time or money. Family, friends, work, other hobbies, charities — these all take time. Even if you truly desired to spend three hours per day training with your new gun, it is likely this would have serious negative consequences in other important areas of your life such as relationships and careers.

This is part of why the "false choice" of either pursuing elite performance or doing nothing can be so harmful to, not just you, but also to the whole industry. In fitness, you do not need to run 10 miles per day or choose to do no physical exercise at all. With shooting, even just maintaining the skill and knowledge to load and unload your gun safely, using a consistent process, will place you *way* ahead on the pathway to a lifetime of safe and effective firearms ownership.

Let us assume, however, that you want more than that. You do not want to be a competitive shooter. You do not want to become a commando. You *do* want to gain the skills, knowledge, and ability to have a better than reasonable chance of successfully defending yourself and your family, should a situation ever occur where using gun is necessary to achieve that result. How do you know what to learn? Once you have learned it, how do you maintain it at a reasonable level of proficiency?

Believe it or not, the first question to ask is what you want to do. For example, if you want to play football, you need to learn markedly different skills than if you want to figure skate. It is the same thing in shooting. I cannot answer that question for you. I can, however, provide you with a few things to consider as you seek to answer it for yourself.

Consideration 1: Beware of the gear trap

What you should consider here is that both guns and the accessories and gear that go with them (including holsters!) are tools that require *training and learning* before they can be used effectively. This is especially true in a self-defense situation. It is easy to get caught in an endless cycle of changing guns, changing gear, and changing accessories. Commercially, this is great for the industry and its vendors. Locally, this is not necessarily great for your skills and abilities.

Choose a set of tools that can meet your needs, then learn to use them. If possible, learn to use them before you buy. If something does not work, breaks, or is just not what you want, change it. I am not suggesting that you stick with something you do not like or that does not work simply because it was recommended to you, or you chose it initially. I am, however, pointing out that constantly changing and swapping gear has the potential to have a negative impact on your ability to develop your skills, especially right at the beginning of your journey. It is very difficult to learn to use something when "something" is itself a set of dynamic variables.

Consideration 2: Understand priorities and limitations

I once had a prospective student who was very concerned about security at his church. He and others were considering forming a volunteer church security team. He wanted primarily to be able to stop a gunman, should the worst happen. He also wanted to carry only a very small revolver in a manner that would make it virtually inaccessible to him within a reasonable timeframe and stated that he thought he would only use it at very close range (arm's length or less).

I started asking him questions and pointed out that attaining a reasonable chance of stopping a gunman in a church security role will almost certainly require more than an arms-length skillset. It will also, therefore, require a pistol that can provide the capability of hitting a gunman from a reasonable distance.

He stated that he wanted a really small gun, carried in very deep cover (which would make it more difficult to retrieve) because he would be in church and needed to make sure no one could possibly see that he had a gun with him. I asked him why this mattered, since he would be legally carrying a pistol as part of a church-sanctioned armed security team. I also asked him why he would carry a weapon for the purposes of saving people's lives, then carry something that made stopping the threat in most conceivable instances unlikely — and carry it in such as way so as to make it virtually impossible to access it fast enough to save a life.

This prospective student is not a dumb person. In fact, he is highly intelligent. His problem was not a lack of smarts, nor even tactical understanding. Rather it was a series of unresolved, conflicting priorities that were combined with a failure to recognize the limitations that are inherent with each piece of equipment.

This issue is actually *very* common, even among skilled and experienced armed professionals. In fact, in my experience the vast majority of arguments and disagreements in tactical environments (between people on the same side of the conflict at least) are rooted in a misalignment of priorities. Sometimes ego also plays a role, as people can refuse to acknowledge and accept that they (or their favorite gear!) are subject to limitations.

As simply a factual matter, everything has limitations. Even the best tool in the world is going to be ill-suited for some jobs. The most skilled person in the world at one thing might very well be a bumbling novice at another. Take the time to understand your own priorities (not everything can be a priority). Also take the time to acknowledge that everything has limitations and that in stressful, self-defense situations, things tend to go wrong.

Consideration Three: Know yourself

It is a fundamental human response to deny the presence, and possibility, of unpleasant things that we cannot control. Sometimes, however, things bubble to the surface fast enough, or loud enough, that we cannot ignore them any longer. We can no longer put them into the mental category of, *That won't happen to me. I'll be fine.*

When this happens, we often take subsequent action. However, it is instructive to understand that what we often *really* want in these cases is to place the problem back into a category we can ignore psychologically. We are often much less interested in addressing the problem itself and far more concerned with returning to a mental state where we can, once again, ignore the problem, pretend it doesn't exist, and move on with our lives.

When I was working as a security provider overseas, on one occasion a coalition helicopter was shot down over a city that my security team supported. Unsure what to do, the powers that be fretted about the possibility that this could happen to aircraft directly supporting our operation. Though we had all been working in a war zone for several years, suddenly a risk that had been present the entire time became unacceptable — simply because it finally happened to somebody.

Eventually, the need to resume operations became pressing, and management settled on a solution. From that point forward, armed security personnel would be stationed on all aircraft flights near that city. How did this reduce our risk of getting shot down? It did not. In fact, it only would have increased the casualty rate if we had been shot out of the sky.

However, that wasn't the point. The action was not about solving the problem of aircraft getting shot down. The action was about solving the problem that the executives could no longer pretend that flying aircraft in a warzone was not inherently risky. Adding security people onboard allowed them to mentally "check the block" and put the problem back in a box of psychological comfort.

If you are brand new to guns and are reading this book in 2021, there is a decent chance that you purchased a gun for the first time in 2020. It was certainly a year for the record books. As if a world-wide pandemic was not enough, protests, riots, a retreat of law enforcement in many areas of the country, a messy trainwreck of an election—all of these things added to chaos, stress and uncertainty. 2020 also highlighted for many people the idea that the police may not be able to protect citizens all of the time. As a result, more people bought guns than perhaps during any year in the history of the U.S.

But, what was the *real* goal? If you are in this

category, was it to gain the ability to protect self and family against lethal threats? Or, was it to gain the ability to stop thinking about the possibility of lethal threats and resume some semblance of normalcy?

Neither answer is wrong. The answer simply is. Accepting risk is one of the ways we can fundamentally deal with it, and each of us does this all the time. There is nothing inherently wrong with it. I would encourage you, however, to strive to be honest with yourself. If you know what problem you are actually trying to solve, it will make your decision-making about how best to solve it far more effective.

Consideration Four: Prepare for bad, hope for good

I assume that most readers will be familiar with the concept of Murphy's Law, summed up by the adage, *What can go wrong, will go wrong.* From the perspective of priorities and training, how you choose to learn and train, and what equipment you choose to learn to use and own, can have long-lasting consequences on your ability to solve problems. Said another way, you cannot put seven shots into a six-shot revolver and if you only prepare to solve a three yard problem, you probably cannot solve a problem at five yards.

Choosing to assume that your self-defense situation (should it ever occur) will fall within a certain set of parameters has the potential to be a mistake with long-term consequences. This is not about always prepping for the worst case (although there's certainly nothing wrong with preparedness). You, hopefully, do not need to assume that the end of the world has arrived and thus prepare to live out the remainder of your life in a dystopian war zone.

However, it is likewise suboptimal to assume that the limit of bad things that could happen to you stop at personal crime inflicted by a single, unskilled, low-level criminal opportunist. Assume bad is possible and reasonably prepare for it. Hope for the best to happen.

Consideration Five:

Match your skill acquisition with your goals

Firearms instructors Karl Rehn and John Daub recently published an excellent book, *Strategies and Standards for Defensive Handgun Training.* The book contains a wealth of information and perspective and, in one of its chapters, discusses the popularity of various training programs across the country. Among the most popular? "Tactical Carbine." Much less popular are courses with handgun skills that are more likely applicable to the average person's daily needs.

Please do not interpret this as criticism of you, or anyone else, for pursuing skills with a carbine. I am a supporter of this for a variety of reasons. I am simply pointing out that, in environments where limited time and resources to invest exist, a big part of making training efficient and effective is choosing to focus training and practice the core fundamentals that will get you to your goal.

CHAPTER FOURTEEN:

TRAINING FOR THE
REAL WORLD

In this chapter I want to briefly explore something that is very near and dear to me: training for performance in the real world. It is accurate to say that the training industry does not *currently* do a very good job at this across the industry and a big part of the reason is a lack of appropriate training tools that are fit for purpose.

Real world tactical and self-defense environments involve complex, rapidly changing, situations with lots of visual and audible stimulus, context, and important decisions that need to be made—right now. In contrast, most training environments involve conducting pre-defined drills on static pieces of paper or steel that require either no decision-making or, in rare cases during "advanced" training, extremely simplistic, binary choices. Occasionally, video simulations or scenarios with role players are also an option.

From the perspective of the brain, you can think of training for real world performance as being very much like designing and building electrical circuitry for a specific purpose. In fact, that is *exactly* what training effectively for real world performance is. It is the development of circuitry in the brain through repetitive performance of the mental processes and physical skills required. The trouble is, we have never had a good way to use most of the relevant circuitry, including visual assessment and decision-making, during the vast majority of firearms training.

I am happy to report that, as of this writing, my Products and Technology team at Building Shooters has solved this problem. We have been hard at work developing a solution since the publication of *Building Shooters* in 2016. Later this year we will be launching a new product line. We call it the **NURO™ Shooting System** and it will fundamentally change firearms and tactical training forever. These tools are available for a limited availability pre-order now on a first come, first serve basis and should be commercially available at the end of 2021 or in early 2022.

NURO™ is designed around how the human brain works and learns (hence its name). We specifically built a system that would be available at consumer and discretionary budget price points, so it will permit *everyone* to integrate the full spectrum of relevant neurological circuitry into every aspect of a firearms training program. Applications range from dryfire in a basement to live-fire on a lane range, to close quarters battle and hostage rescue training for specialized teams of armed professionals.

By incorporating NURO™ into every aspect of training, the industry finally has the capability to be able to add the circuitry for visual skills, thinking, and decision-making (among others) into the networks that comprise shooting skill application. To learn more about the NURO™ Shooting System, and the research behind its design, please see my book of the same name.

With respect to specifics in terms of skills for defensive firearms use, the following sample curriculum is contained within my 2017 book *Mentoring Shooters* (along with instructor notes that are not included here). While this outline is by no means exhaustive, it does cover the general minimal defensive firearms skills for concealed carry.

This is not a book about shooting skills or tactics, therefore not everything here may make sense to you at this time if you are in the intended audience for this book. I include it as a general guideline for your reference regarding the scope and breadth of skills and knowledge that are involved in training for self-defense firearms use.

Sample Defensive Handgun Curriculum

Lesson 1:

Teach: N/A

Prime: firearms basics, safety rules, inserting/ removing magazine, locking slide to the rear

Enhance: N/A

Lesson 2:

Teach: firearms basics, safety rules, inserting/ removing magazine, locking slide to the rear

Prime: loading/unloading magazine, loading/ unloading pistol

Enhance: N/A

Lesson 3:

Teach: loading/unloading magazine, loading/ unloading pistol

Prime: shooting grip, static sight picture, trigger manipulation

Enhance: firearms basics, safety rules, inserting/ removing magazine, locking slide to the rear

Lesson 4:

Live Fire Recommended

Teach: shooting grip, static sight picture, trigger manipulation

Prime: recoil management, trigger reset, shooting cycle, situational awareness

Enhance: firearms basics, safety rules, inserting/ removing magazine, locking slide to the rear, loading/unloading magazine, loading/ unloading pistol

Lesson 5:

Live Fire Recommended

Teach: recoil management, trigger reset, shooting cycle, situational awareness

Prime: pistol presentation (dry only), flash sight picture

Enhance: firearms basics, safety rules, inserting/ removing magazine, locking slide to the rear, loading/unloading magazine, loading/ unloading pistol, shooting grip, static sight picture, trigger manipulation

Lesson 6:

Teach: pistol presentation, flash sight picture

Prime: emergency reload, firearm-safety recommendations

Enhance: firearms basics, safety rules, inserting/removing magazine, locking slide to the rear, loading/unloading magazine, loading/unloading pistol, shooting grip, static sight picture, trigger manipulation, recoil management, trigger reset, shooting cycle, situational awareness

Lesson 7:

Teach: emergency reload, firearm-safety recommendations

Prime: soft-malfunction clearance, use-of-force decision-making

Enhance: firearms basics, safety rules, inserting/removing magazine, locking slide to the rear, loading/unloading magazine, loading/unloading pistol, shooting grip, static sight picture, trigger manipulation, recoil management, trigger reset, shooting cycle, situational awareness, pistol presentation, flash sight picture

Lesson 8:

Live Fire Recommended

Teach: soft-malfunction clearance, use-of-force decision-making

Prime: mobility (related to positioning/ retention), retention shooting position

Enhance: firearms basics, safety rules, inserting/removing magazine, locking slide to the rear, loading/unloading magazine, loading/unloading pistol, shooting grip, static sight picture, trigger manipulation, recoil management, trigger reset, shooting cycle, situational awareness, pistol presentation, flash sight picture, emergency reload, firearm-safety recommendations

Lesson 9:

Teach: mobility (related to positioning/retention), retention shooting position

Prime: cover garments, concealed presentation and reload

Enhance: firearms basics, safety rules, inserting/removing magazine, locking slide to the rear, loading/unloading magazine, loading/unloading pistol, shooting grip, static sight picture, trigger manipulation, recoil management, trigger reset, shooting cycle, situational awareness, pistol presentation, flash sight picture, emergency reload, firearm-safety recommendations, soft-malfunction clearance, use-of-force decision-making

Lesson 10:

Teach: cover garments, concealed presentation and reload

Prime: hard-malfunction clearance

Enhance: firearms basics, safety rules, inserting/removing magazine, locking slide to the rear, loading/unloading magazine, loading/unloading pistol, shooting grip, static sight picture, trigger manipulation, recoil management, trigger reset, shooting cycle, situational awareness, pistol presentation, flash sight picture, emergency reload, firearm-safety recommendations, soft-malfunction clearance, use-of-force decision-making, mobility (related to positioning/retention), retention shooting position

Lesson 11:

Live Fire Recommended

Teach: hard-malfunction clearance

Prime: spontaneous defense, pistol retention

Enhance: firearms basics, safety rules, inserting/removing magazine, locking slide to the rear, loading/unloading magazine, loading/unloading pistol, shooting grip, static sight picture, trigger manipulation, recoil management, trigger reset, shooting cycle, situational awareness, pistol presentation, flash sight picture, emergency reload, firearm-safety recommendations, soft-malfunction clearance, use-of-force decision-making, mobility (related to positioning/retention), retention shooting position, cover garments, concealed presentation and reload

Lesson 12:

Teach: spontaneous defense, pistol retention

Prime: deterrence, verbal challenge, phone/communication access

Enhance: firearms basics, safety rules, inserting/removing magazine, locking slide to the rear, loading/unloading magazine, loading/unloading pistol, shooting grip, static sight picture, trigger manipulation, recoil management, trigger reset, shooting cycle, situational awareness, pistol presentation, flash sight picture, emergency reload, firearm-safety recommendations, soft-malfunction clearance, use-of-force decision-making, mobility (related to positioning/retention), retention shooting position, cover garments, concealed presentation and reload, hard-malfunction clearance

If this list looks intimidating to you, it should not. Anyone can learn this. Firearms are relatively easy to operate effectively for self-defense purposes. However, this does not mean that training and practice are not required.

As I have said repeatedly throughout this book,

attaining competence with a firearm for self-defense is not an immediate event. It will not happen in a day and it cannot be purchased. Money can help with resources; however, it ultimately is not that type of investment that is required. The investment is in properly structured time and effort.

This said, it is absolutely not a requirement for you to dedicate the remainder of your life to mastering combative firearms skills. You will certainly be more prepared if you do so. However, a moderate investment to *learn right* upfront followed by some minimal periodic upkeep and maintenance will make you a very safe, competent shooter with the capability to defend yourself and your family.

Regardless of whether or not you eventually choose to integrate NURO™ into your personal training program, when training for the real world, remember from the previous section of this book how the human brain learns. You cannot accomplish it all in one day, nor in two. Take your time at the beginning. Build the relevant skills — neural circuitry — at the same pace your brain is capable of constructing it. Once again, it is all about the brain!

CHAPTER FIFTEEN:

TACTICS, TECHNIQUES, PROCEDURES – A CONSUMER'S GUIDE

The final thing that I want to discuss in this book is "tactics." This is a word that is often thrown around. Unfortunately, this frequently happens without much understanding of what it means. Humorously, sometimes it is easy to forget that "tactics" does not simply refer to covering oneself with earth-toned clothing, molle loops, and Velcro.

I want to take some time to set this straight because tactics are important. I will start by defining what the word *actually* means. In a nutshell, tactics is problem solving. It requires understanding your own limitations and capabilities, as well as those of any potential adversaries. It then involves understanding your objective, followed by applying your own capabilities against, preferably, your adversary's limitations to accomplish the objective within the environment that the confrontation occurs in.

If this sounds a bit cerebral and somewhat familiar after reading the previous chapters in this book—you are correct! Tactics are in the mind, not in the muscle. The muscle simply carries out techniques. If you fully understand everything that is in this book prior to this chapter, then you most likely have a relatively good understanding of tactics, whether you would have labeled it "tactics" before reading this or not.

Good tactics heavily depend upon the variables involved. Is it good tactics to swim across a lake to conduct an assault on a military objective? I don't know. Can you swim? Are there alligators in the lake? Can you climb out of the lake on the other side?

This is, of course, hyperbole for the purposes of this book. However, it should highlight the point. Tactics are about problem solving. If you do not define and understand yourself, the adversary, the terrain, and the objective, you cannot discuss tactics.

Nevertheless, it is not uncommon to encounter classes, writings, videos, or training that purport to teach tactics without the requisite background information to do so. For example, suppose you were to attend a class called, "Low Light Tactics." In it, perhaps you learn several different methods to use a handheld flashlight with a handgun, as well as several methods for using a flashlight to navigate barriers such as walls and doors. At the end of the class, suppose you have learned to hold a flashlight two different ways. You have also learned two different ways of manipulating a handheld light while moving towards a doorway or barricade.

Are these tactics? The answer is no. Without information such as what environment you are in, who the adversary is, and what you are trying to accomplish, you can only practice skills that may (or may not) be relevant when *actual* tactics are involved. You have learned *techniques* in this hypothetical class. This is not a bad thing. It is just worthwhile to understand that there is a difference.

If this seems to you like I am needlessly splitting hairs, you have a point with respect to the terminology. Cleverly defining words ultimately does little good. While I do want to provide the correct definitions here for informational purposes, "gotcha" word games are not my intent. I would also advise you against quibbling too much with others (especially instructors!) on the subject.

After all, "tactics" is a good search engine keyword and marketing matters in any commercial endeavor. The primary reason I am taking the time to address this is because the *concepts* in this discussion are extremely important to you as a consumer.

Consider the following example: During my time in the Navy, one of the security force members who worked for me learned a flashlight technique called *strobing* during a training class. In this context, strobing means rapidly flashing the light on and off. There are some benefits to this lighting technique in combative environments. For example, it can disrupt an adversary's ability to tracking your exact location or pace of movement from an adjoining room when you are inside a building.

Believing that he had learned "low light tactics" rather than simply a flashlight technique, this sailor pulled his flashlight out in the middle of a field, in the woods, at night, while approaching what he thought might be a potential human threat — and began strobing. By doing so he gave away the position of his team to anyone within several hundred yards, compromised his team's natural night vision (gained after spending several hours in the dark) and threw away any potential tactical advantage his team might have had from being unseen (at least up until that point) by any adversary.

Fortunately, this event occurred during a training exercise and no real harm was done. It also hopefully illustrates to you why these concepts matter. Techniques (such as flashlight strobing) are important. They are used during tactics (i.e., problem solving). However, tactics and techniques are markedly different things. Just because a technique can have great tactical value does not mean using the technique is good tactics! While the specific terminology is not overly important, understanding these different concepts is very important.

A third, related, term that I want to briefly define here is *procedure*. This is a common term and is probably something you use in your workplace. In the firearms and tactical world, this usually refers to a collection or sequence of techniques or methods that an organization approves formally as a standard. For example, a police department may have a specific sequence of events that are expected when an officer arrives at the scene of a violent crime. This may include things such as making a radio call with certain information included (time, location, etc.), and waiting for a second officer to arrive before entering a building.

In military, law enforcement, and security settings, information related to these three concepts are often combined into documents called *Tactics, Techniques, and Procedures* (TTPs for short), or, sometimes, *Tactics, Techniques, Policies, and Procedures* (TTPPs) when organizational policy (such as a police department's policy for use of force) is also included. This is unlikely to be relevant to you. However, does help explain one contributing factor to why these terms can sometimes be used interchangeably (and incorrectly).

Understanding the differences is important. For example, learning and practicing multiple *techniques* can be a treacherous slope to navigate when the differing techniques are fundamental mechanics and are *used to accomplish the same objective.*

Suppose, for example, that you were to learn and practice several different methods for gripping a handgun with two hands. The task is holding the gun. The objective is controlling it to allow you to place accurate rounds on target quickly. During a high-stress, real-world situation, which of the different techniques would you use? Would you, *could you* even perform any of them correctly when under stress?

The answers to these questions are difficult because

you would have learned competing techniques to do the same thing. Gripping the gun could be part of a rapid response in a very stressful environment (such as an attacker charging you with a knife or a home invader kicking down your front door).

There are multiple ways to grip a gun that can work for self-defense. However, you cannot perform more than one technique at a time. Learning and practicing multiple techniques has little practical value. In fact, this may even interfere with your ability to grip a handgun effectively.

Importantly, this relates to your selection of technique and what skills you choose to practice. It also relates to what classes you take, who you choose as instructors, and what written / online content you consume. As a general rule you should only seek to learn and practice a single technique for accomplishing a specific *fundamental task and objective*. This is especially important if it will be performed during a self-defense situation.

This does not mean that there are not multiple techniques that can work. In fact, there is usually more than one way to do most skills that are adequate for self-defense. It does mean, however, that you should pick instructors and sources of information that are both valid and grounded in the applications that you wish to pursue (such as competition, self-defense, etc.).

By choosing wisely at the beginning, you can ensure that you do not learn and practice techniques that do NOT work for your intended applications. For example, some techniques that may be adequate for self-defense will fail miserably in competition, while some techniques will work fine for both. If you learn suboptimal things up front—things that you then need to go unlearn—it will make your path to competency far more difficult and time consuming than it needs to be. What is the best way to avoid this? Choose a good instructor and a good source of information.

With respect to procedures and tactics though, this same concept does NOT typically apply. For example, there are several different ways to approach, and move through a door. These types of sequences can be considered procedures, or higher-level techniques (as opposed to fundamental techniques such as gripping a gun). Each of these different procedures has advantages and disadvantages—choosing which one to apply should be based on factors such as the objective, environment, adversary, etc.

Do you want to search the building for something?

Or do you want to solve a specific and acute problem in the building? If you find what you are searching for, what are you going to do? Will you approach? Will you shoot? Will you be shot at? Will you back away and leave the building? Understanding the answers to these types of questions will help you determine which advantages are critical to your success, and which disadvantages are most (or least) likely to hurt you. These answers will inform your choice about what to do — this is the essence of tactics.

Unlike gripping the gun — a more-or-less consistently performed skill to accomplish a single objective — the more complex skill sequence, or procedure, of moving through a door may be used to support accomplishing any number of different objectives. It may be performed going through many different types of doors, in many different lighting conditions, with many different sets of circumstances involved. Everything will have its own advantages and drawbacks. Having multiple options to apply to maximize the chances of success can be extremely beneficial in a tactical environment.

This is not intended to be a lesson on tactics. I simply seek to explain the terms and provide a set of considerations for you to use as you choose instructors and sources of information. Given the subject matter, however, I do believe that it is important to make one specific point.

Decision-making is usually the key to prevailing in tactical environments and indecision is a killer. In most cases, mediocre decisions and tactics will ultimately get the job done if they are performed well and in a timely manner. Perfect decisions that never get made will always fail. Please do not misinterpret this chapter as advocating for "paralysis by analysis" in tactical environments.

The Aiming Controversy – A Technique Discussion

To conclude this book, I am going to provide my opinion on one specific area of fundamental technique performance. As I said in Chapter 2, I purposely did not write a "how to shoot" book. There are many good sources for that information, some of which I have provided links to within these pages. I also highly recommend that you attempt to find a good local instructor to help guide you.

Back to the technique: This is an issue that I think is incredibly important. In fact, I wrote a book about it, titled *Hitting in Combat*. The subject is aiming; the book seeks specifically to answer the question: *Is it possible to aim in a gunfight?* Please read *Hitting in Combat* to see the full details and the scientific references. However, I feel that it would be irresponsible of me to completely ignore this here.

Some instructors believe strongly in using visual techniques to aim that involve the sights on the gun. Others believe that while this typically produces the best results on a paper target, it is nevertheless impossible to do under the stress and chaos of a real gunfight. These instructors and shooters therefore believe that "combat shooting" should *not* involve use of the gun's sights. Instead, the human body's natural ability to align itself and understand its relative position in space is used to point the gun and hit the target.

This topic is an area of long-standing controversy. It also has a fascinating historical context, going back to before World War Two. Here I will be both brief and blunt. Any assertion that it is impossible to aim under stress or in a gunfight is grade A baloney. This is quite simply false. Many people do it — therefore it cannot be impossible.

What I do believe to be true, however, is that *how shooters are trained*, and how they practice during their first few exposures to the subject matter, are tremendously important with respect to a student's long-term potential. A person trained NOT to use the sights during his or her early exposure to shooting will find it (more or less) impossible to aim in a gunfight. Even worse, he or she will also find it virtually impossible *to learn* to aim in a gunfight.

On the other hand, a person who learns combatively relevant (as opposed to target shooting techniques) methods of visually aiming *first* will not only learn to aim in a gunfight, he or she will also be perfectly capable of learning and applying non-visually-aimed-shooting techniques during those situations when they are the best method of getting the job done.

Shooting without the use of sights early-on makes it almost impossible to learn and consolidate aiming the gun visually within procedural memory. If you choose to train this way at the beginning, you are embracing a significant accuracy and distance limitation in your future and should not count on ever being able to hit a human being at any distance exceeding a few paces. The choice is yours — but the results may be permanent. Choose wisely.

THANK YOU AND JOIN US!

Thank you for reading this book. Welcome to gun ownership—if you are a new gun owner. I hope you have found the information in these pages unique among the volumes of information available to you, as well as informative and useful. I also hope that you have taken with you some items that have made you safer and that will contribute to making your development as a shooter more efficient, more effective and (again) safer that it would have otherwise been.

If you found this book valuable, please take a moment and **post a short review of it on Amazon** to help us spread the word about the value of brain-based training.

If you have not yet done so, please also take this opportunity to sign up for access to our newsletter and our free comprehensive video series on gun safety and gun handling fundamentals. Join us in working to make the industry, and society as a whole, a better, safer place. Access is available at:

https://www.buildingshooters.com/free

MORE FROM BUILDING SHOOTERS

If you would like to learn more about firearms and tactical training, applied neuroscience, and how the firearms training industry can improve, please consider the following additional titles from Building Shooters:

Building Shooters: Applying Neuroscience Research to Tactical Training Design and Training Delivery

Mentoring Shooters: The Gun Owner's Guide to Building a Firearms Culture of Safety and Personal Responsibility

On Training: Volume 1 - Selected Essays

On Training: Volume 2 – Selected Essays

Hitting in Combat: The Brain Science of Training to Win Gunfights – Available June 2021

NURO: A Brain-Based Analysis of Tactical Training and the Basis of Design for the World's Most Capable Tactical Training System - Available May 2021

Building Shooters' books are available at **www.buildingshooters.com**, on Amazon.com, and from other online book retailers.